core belief™

Bible Study Series
for senior high

WHY Jesus Christ MATTERS

Group®
Loveland, Colorado

Why Jesus Christ Matters

Core Belief Bible Study Series

Visit our Web site: **www.grouppublishing.com**

Credits

Editors: Lisa Baba Lauffer and Karl Leuthauser
Managing Editor: Michael D. Warden
Chief Creative Officer: Joani Schultz
Copy Editor: Debbie Gowensmith
Art Director: Lisa Chandler
Cover Art Director: Helen H. Lannis
Cover Designer/Assistant Art Director: Bill Fisher
Computer Graphic Artist: Kari K. Monson
Photographer: Craig DeMartino
Illustrator: Ray Tollison
Production Manager: Gingar Kunkel

ISBN 0-7644-0875-5

10 9 8 7 6 5 4 3 06 05 04 03 02 01

Printed in the United States of America.

core belief™

Bible Study Series

for senior high

contents:

the Core Belief: Jesus Christ

He's the Son of God yet is completely God. He became fully human but was still fully God. How do we reconcile all the paradoxes Jesus presents to us? We'll never figure them out here on earth. But we do know this: God came to the earth he created to redeem his people. Jesus Christ lived, was tempted with everything Satan could throw at him, and still lived a perfectly sinless life. Yet he paid the price for all the world's sin anyway. He faced death and conquered it. By doing so, he saved us all.

What can we do in return? Nothing . . . except give Jesus our whole lives, following him as our Lord and as our example of how to live. He doesn't leave us to flounder on our own. He mediates between us and God, defending us whenever we sin because he already paid the penalty. And someday he's coming back to take us home.

From these studies about Jesus Christ, students should learn not only about Jesus' life, death, and resurrection, but also about his participation in their daily lives—and how they can respond to him.

the Helpful Stuff

ents:

the Studies

Jesus Christ as a Core Christian Belief

Your kids are constantly bombarded by false images of Christianity and of Jesus. Young people around them are experimenting with all kinds of religious beliefs—or are rejecting the idea of religion as a whole. Tolerance for everyone's perspective is the law of the land. And yet traditional beliefs about Jesus are often questioned and ridiculed by students and even teachers at school.

The result of this pseudoreligious "melting pot" is that many Christian teenagers have difficulty seeing the value or uniqueness of Christianity. That's why it's critical that your young people understand who Jesus is. They need to know what he came to earth to do and why he did it. They need to see the love that prompted God to send his Son to die on earth so that they might have eternal life.

These studies will help your kids develop a clear understanding of the nature and purpose of Jesus Christ. First they'll compare their own tendencies toward teenage **rebellion** with Jesus' holy rebellion against the religious leaders of his day; they'll discover that Jesus is a "holy rebel" they can follow.

In the second study, kids will focus on **comparing religions** by comparing Jesus with the founders of two other world religions: Islam and Buddhism. Through this comparison, kids will discover that Jesus was not just a man like other religious leaders. He is God, and he became human to save us all.

The third study directs kids to explore **Jesus' power,** to examine how he demonstrated his greatest strength when he died on the cross, and to recognize how that power still reaches out to us today.

Finally, kids will turn their attention inward to focus on **self-image.** They'll discover that they can find encouragement and self-worth in knowing that Jesus is always with us and always understands our hearts.

Your kids need to encounter the real Jesus—and discover how following him sets them apart from all religions or beliefs. To do that, we must turn to the only totally reliable source of information about him: the Bible. There we can read about the true Jesus—the one who loves us and died for our sins so that we can live abundantly and eternally with him.

For a more comprehensive look at this Core Christian Belief, read Group's ***Get Real: Making Core Christian Beliefs Relevant to Teenagers.***

DEPTH FINDER

HOW THE BIBLE DESCRIBES JESUS CHRIST

To help you effectively guide your kids toward this Core Christian Belief, use these overviews as a launching point for a more in-depth study of Jesus Christ.

- **Jesus is God.** In a way we can't fully understand, Jesus is God. He is one with the Father and with the Holy Spirit. He has always existed, but he also lived as a human for a time. While living on earth, he demonstrated that he has the power and authority of God. His resurrection and ascension to heaven are further proof of his deity (Micah 5:2; Matthew 1:18-25; Mark 2:8-12; John 1:1-2, 14; 10:30; Acts 1:8-11; Colossians 2:9).
- **Jesus took part in Creation.** Having always been God, Jesus was there when the earth was "empty and had no form," and all things were created through him (Genesis 1:1-2; John 1:3; 1 Corinthians 8:6; Colossians 1:16-17).
- **Jesus became human.** Without becoming any less God, Jesus also became fully human. His humanity and divinity are intertwined in a way we can't explain. He was born the child of Mary, having been conceived by the Holy Spirit. Jesus lived on earth, growing from a child to a man and experiencing the same temptations and struggles we do. He got tired, hungry, and thirsty. And he died (Matthew 1:18-25; Luke 2:52; John 4:6; Galatians 4:4; Philippians 2:5-8; 1 Timothy 2:5; Hebrews 4:15).
- **Jesus is the Messiah.** "Christ" is the Greek word that corresponds to the Hebrew word "Messiah." Jesus Christ is the Messiah promised by God in the Old Testament (Matthew 16:16; Mark 14:61-62; John 1:40-41; 4:25-26; Acts 2:36; 9:22).
- **Jesus is sinless.** As the God-man on earth, Jesus was totally obedient to the Father. Though he was tempted in every way, he never sinned (John 8:46; Romans 5:19; 2 Corinthians 5:21; Hebrews 4:15; 1 Peter 2:22).
- **Jesus is our Savior.** Jesus' death on the cross paid the penalty for our sins. His resurrection guarantees eternal life for all who believe in him. Through Jesus' death and resurrection, we can be freed from our sins, have a personal relationship with God, and have eternal life with him (Isaiah 53; Matthew 1:21; Luke 19:9-10; John 3:14-18; Acts 5:30-31; Romans 5:6-11).

- **Jesus is our example.** While living on earth, Jesus taught and modeled how we are to live. His compassion for people, his intolerance of injustice, and his obedience and devotion to the Father are examples we should seek to follow (John 13:1-15; Ephesians 5:1-2; 1 Peter 1:14-15; 2:21-23; 1 John 2:4-6).
- **Jesus is Lord.** "Lord" is the term Jews of Jesus' day used to refer to God, but it was also used to refer to earthly masters or rulers. The early Christians used it to refer to Jesus, probably incorporating both of those ideas. Jesus is ruler over all. He is to be the master of Christians' lives and is deserving of all our worship (Romans 10:12-13; 14:8-12; 1 Corinthians 8:6; Philippians 2:9-11; 1 Timothy 6:13-16).
- **Jesus is our Intercessor.** Jesus is the one mediator between God and humans. Seated at the right hand of the Father, Jesus is always there to defend us when we sin. Because he paid the penalty of sin, we who have faith in him are no longer guilty (Romans 8:34-39; 1 Timothy 2:5-6; Hebrews 7:23-25; 1 John 2:1-2).
- **Jesus will return.** When the time is right, Jesus will return to earth to take those who are his to live with him forever. It will be a time of judgment and of reward. We don't know when that time will be, and we aren't certain of all the details surrounding that time, but we do know that he will return and that it will be a joyous time for Christians (Matthew 16:27; 24:36-42; John 14:1-3; 1 Thessalonians 4:13-18; Revelation 22:12-13).

CORE CHRISTIAN BELIEF OVERVIEW

Here are the twenty-four Core Christian Belief categories that form the backbone of Core Belief Bible Study Series:

The Nature of God	Jesus Christ	The Holy Spirit
Humanity	Evil	Suffering
Creation	The Spiritual Realm	The Bible
Salvation	Spiritual Growth	Personal Character
God's Justice	Sin & Forgiveness	The Last Days
Love	The Church	Worship
Authority	Prayer	Family
Service	Relationships	Sharing Faith

Look for Group's Core Belief Bible Study Series books in these other Core Christian Beliefs!

about core belief

Bible Study Series
for senior high

Think for a moment about your young people. When your students walk out of your youth program after they graduate from junior high or high school, what do you want them to know? What foundation do you want them to have so they can make wise choices?

You probably want them to know the essentials of the Christian faith. You want them to base everything they do on the foundational truths of Christianity. Are you meeting this goal?

If you have any doubt that your kids will walk into adulthood knowing and living by the tenets of the Christian faith, then you've picked up the right book. All the books in Group's Core Belief Bible Study Series encourage young people to discover the essentials of Christianity and to put those essentials into practice. Let us explain...

What Is Group's Core Belief Bible Study Series?

Group's Core Belief Bible Study Series is a biblically in-depth study series for junior high and senior high teenagers. This Bible study series utilizes four defining commitments to create each study. These "plumb lines" provide structure and continuity for every activity, study, project, and discussion. They are:

- **A Commitment to Biblical Depth**—Core Belief Bible Study Series is founded on the belief that kids not only *can* understand the deeper truths of the Bible but also *want* to understand them. Therefore, the activities and studies in this series strive to explain the "why" behind every truth we explore. That way, kids learn principles, not just rules.
- **A Commitment to Relevance**—Most kids aren't interested in abstract theories or doctrines about the universe. They want to know how to live successfully right now, today, in the heat of problems they can't ignore. Because of this, each study connects a real-life need with biblical principles that speak directly to that need. This study series finally bridges the gap between Bible truths and the real-world issues kids face.
- **A Commitment to Variety**—Today's young people have been raised in a sound bite world. They demand variety. For that reason, no two meetings in this study series are shaped exactly the same.
- **A Commitment to Active and Interactive Learning**—Active learning is learning by doing. Interactive learning simply takes active learning a step further by having kids teach each other what they've learned. It's a process that helps kids internalize and remember their discoveries.

For a more detailed description of these concepts, see the section titled "Why Active and Interactive Learning Works With Teenagers" beginning on page 57.

So how can you accomplish all this in a set of four easy-to-lead Bible studies? By weaving together various "power" elements to produce a fun experience that leaves kids challenged and encouraged.

Turn the page to take a look at some of the power elements used in this series.

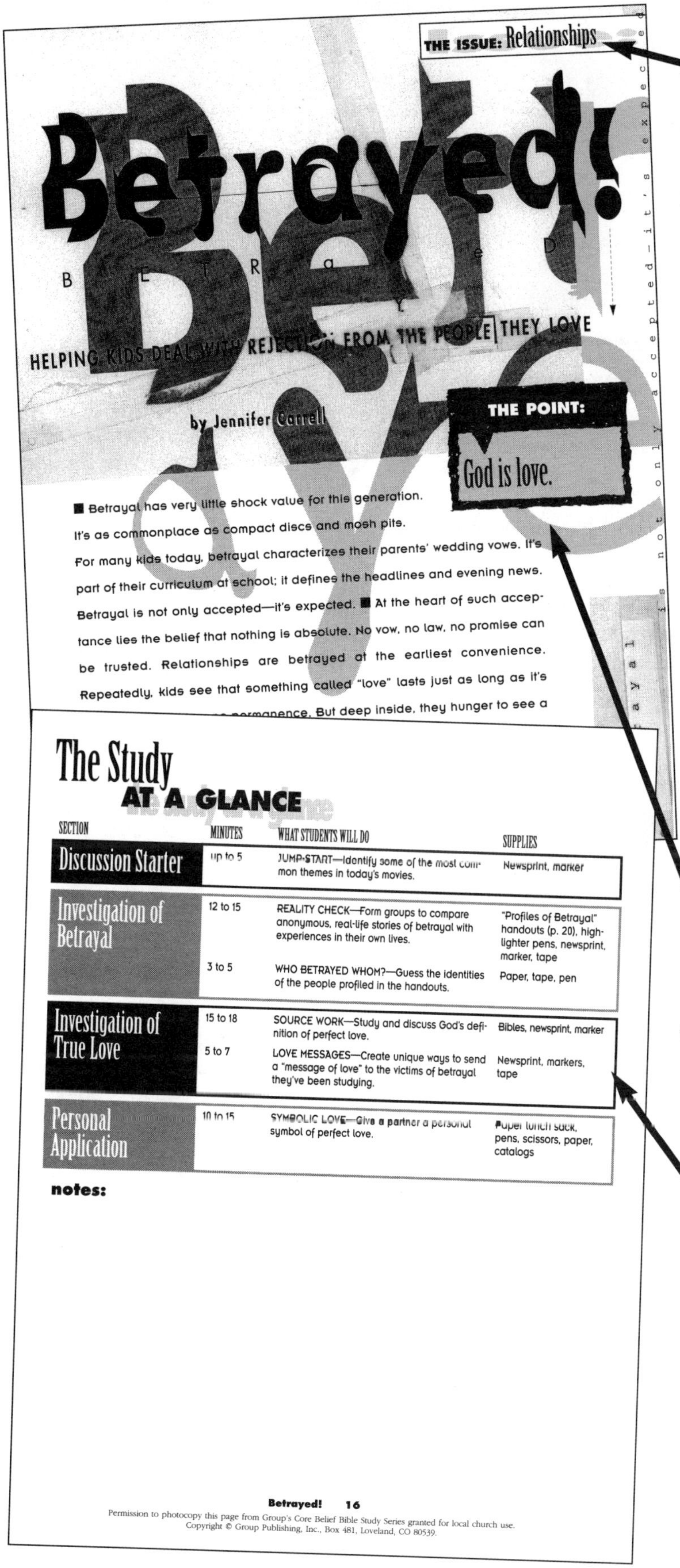

THE ISSUE: Relationships

Betrayed!

HELPING KIDS DEAL WITH REJECTION FROM THE PEOPLE THEY LOVE

by Jennifer Carrell

THE POINT:

God is love.

■ Betrayal has very little shock value for this generation. It's as commonplace as compact discs and mosh pits. For many kids today, betrayal characterizes their parents' wedding vows. It's part of their curriculum at school; it defines the headlines and evening news. Betrayal is not only accepted—it's expected. ■ At the heart of such acceptance lies the belief that nothing is absolute. No vow, no law, no promise can be trusted. Relationships are betrayed at the earliest convenience. Repeatedly, kids see that something called "love" lasts just as long as it's ... permanence. But deep inside, they hunger to see a

The Study AT A GLANCE

SECTION	MINUTES	WHAT STUDENTS WILL DO	SUPPLIES
Discussion Starter	up to 5	JUMP-START—Identify some of the most common themes in today's movies.	Newsprint, marker
Investigation of Betrayal	12 to 15	REALITY CHECK—Form groups to compare anonymous, real-life stories of betrayal with experiences in their own lives.	"Profiles of Betrayal" handouts (p. 20), highlighter pens, newsprint, marker, tape
	3 to 5	WHO BETRAYED WHOM?—Guess the identities of the people profiled in the handouts.	Paper, tape, pen
Investigation of True Love	15 to 18	SOURCE WORK—Study and discuss God's definition of perfect love.	Bibles, newsprint, marker
	5 to 7	LOVE MESSAGES—Create unique ways to send a "message of love" to the victims of betrayal they've been studying.	Newsprint, markers, tape
Personal Application	10 to 15	SYMBOLIC LOVE—Give a partner a personal symbol of perfect love.	Paper lunch sack, pens, scissors, paper, catalogs

notes:

Betrayed! 16

Permission to photocopy this page from Group's Core Belief Bible Study Series granted for local church use. Copyright © Group Publishing, Inc., Box 481, Loveland, CO 80539.

- **A Relevant Topic—**More than ever before, kids live in the now. What matters to them and what attracts their hearts is what's happening in their world at this moment. For this reason, every Core Belief Bible Study focuses on a particular hot topic that kids care about.

- **A Core Christian Belief—**Group's Core Belief Bible Study Series organizes the wealth of Christian truth and experience into twenty-four Core Christian Belief categories. These twenty-four headings act as umbrellas for a collection of detailed beliefs that define Christianity and set it apart from the world and every other religion. Each book in this series features one Core Christian Belief with lessons suited for junior high or senior high students.

  "But," you ask, "won't my kids be bored talking about all these spiritual beliefs?" No way! As a youth leader, you know the value of using hot topics to connect with young people. Ultimately teenagers talk about issues because they're searching for meaning in their lives. They want to find the one equation that will make sense of all the confusing events happening around them. Each Core Belief Bible Study answers that need by connecting a hot topic with a powerful Christian principle. Kids walk away from the study with something more solid than just the shifting ebb and flow of their own opinions. They walk away with a deeper understanding of their Christian faith.

- **The Point—**This simple statement is designed to be the intersection between the Core Christian Belief and the hot topic. Everything in the study ultimately focuses on The Point so that kids study it and allow it time to sink into their hearts.

- **The Study at a Glance—**A quick look at this chart will tell you what kids will do, how long it will take them to do it, and what supplies you'll need to get it done.

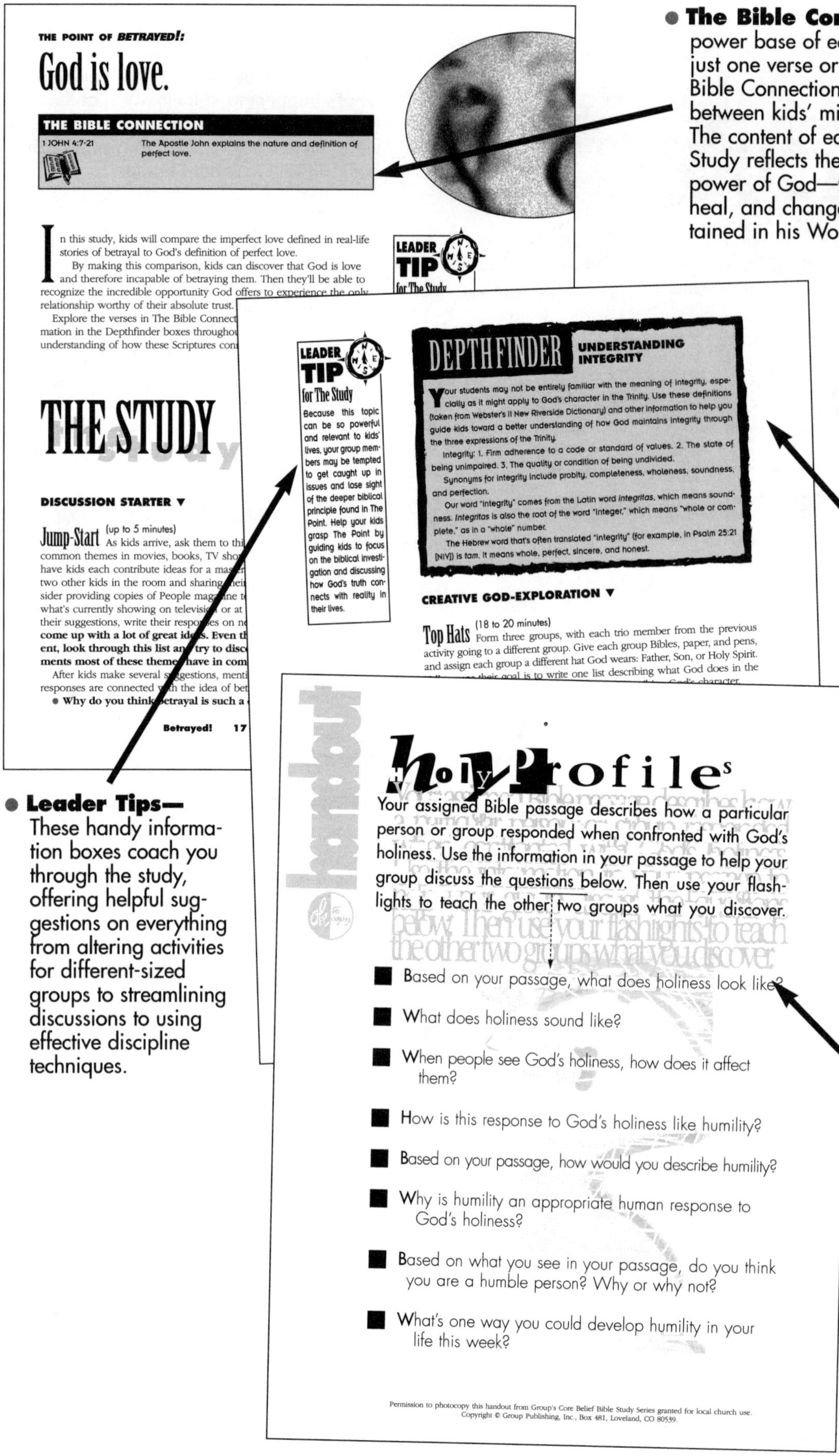

- **The Bible Connection**—This is the power base of each study. Whether it's just one verse or several chapters, The Bible Connection provides the vital link between kids' minds and their hearts. The content of each Core Belief Bible Study reflects the belief that the true power of God—the power to expose, heal, and change kids' lives—is contained in his Word.

- **Depthfinder Boxes**—These informative sidelights located throughout each study add insight into a particular passage, word, historical fact, or Christian doctrine. Depthfinder boxes also provide insight into teen culture, adolescent development, current events, and philosophy.

- **Leader Tips**—These handy information boxes coach you through the study, offering helpful suggestions on everything from altering activities for different-sized groups to streamlining discussions to using effective discipline techniques.

- **Handouts**—Most Core Belief Bible Studies include photocopiable handouts to use with your group. Handouts might take the form of a fun game, a lively discussion starter, or a challenging study page for kids to take home—anything to make your study more meaningful and effective.

The Last Word on Core Belief Bible Studies

Soon after you begin to use Group's Core Belief Bible Study Series, you'll see signs of real growth in your group members. Your kids will gain a deeper understanding of the Bible and of their own Christian faith. They'll see more clearly how a relationship with Jesus affects their daily lives. And they'll grow closer to God.

But that's not all. You'll also see kids grow closer to one another.

That's because this series is founded on the principle that Christian faith grows best in the context of relationship. Each study uses a variety of interactive pairs and small groups and always includes discussion questions that promote deeper relationships. The friendships kids will build through this study series will enable them to grow *together* toward a deeper relationship with God.

Jesus *the* Rebel

by Michael D. Warden

THE POINT:

Jesus is a "holy rebel" you can follow.

■ Teenage rebellion isn't what it used to be. Just look around. You'll see no wild protest marches, no us-vs.-them sit-ins, no long-winded confrontations with the law. Kids today have no need for such pointless rebellious displays. They haven't just changed the rules. They've effectively quit the game. Where kids once proclaimed, "If you don't like authority, fight it," many of today's young people live by a different law: "If you don't like authority, ignore it." This study compares modern teenagers' "rebellion of indifference" with Christ's powerful "targeted rebellion" against the spiritual leaders of his day, and it challenges kids to embrace Jesus as God's example of a "rebel" worthy of their following.

The Study AT A GLANCE

SECTION	MINUTES	WHAT STUDENTS WILL DO	SUPPLIES
Introductions	up to 5	ART WARS—Try to draw two different pictures on the same section of newsprint.	Newsprint, tape, markers
Investigative Study	30 to 35	GOD'S CHOSEN REBEL—Form groups to explore different aspects of Christ's "acts of rebellion," then teach each other what they learned.	Bibles, newsprint, markers
Debriefing and Commitment	up to 10	JESUS AND ME—Talk with a partner about the similarities and differences between Christ's rebellion and their own.	Bibles
	up to 10	HOLY REBELLION—Receive a challenge to channel their rebellion toward following Jesus.	Bibles, "Holy Rebellion" bookmarks (p. 23), pens
Planning Time	up to 5	SERVANT ATTACK—Plan a re-enactment of one of Jesus' rebellious actions by washing people's feet during the church service.	Large bowls, towels, water

notes:

THE POINT OF ***JESUS THE REBEL:***

Jesus is a "holy rebel" you can follow.

THE BIBLE CONNECTION	
LUKE 6:1-11; 7:36-50; JOHN 2:12-22; 13:1-9	In each of these passages, Jesus rebels against the popular thought of his day.
MATTHEW 5:10-12	Jesus voices his approval of people who are persecuted for following him.
JOHN 15:18-20	Jesus warns his disciples not to be surprised if the world rejects them.

In this study, kids will investigate several "rebellious" acts Jesus committed during his life on earth and will compare his positive rebellion with rebellious attitudes in their own lives. As a part of this comparison, kids will work together to plan and commit a positive act of rebellion in their own church.

Through this investigation, kids can realize that their own rebellion can be a godly attribute when it's aimed against the injustice, hypocrisy, and unrighteousness that surrounds them.

Explore the verses in The Bible Connection, then examine the information in the Depthfinder boxes throughout the study to gain a deeper understanding of how these Scriptures connect with your young people.

LEADER TIP for The Study

Whenever you ask groups to discuss a list of questions, write the list on newsprint and tape it to a wall so groups can discuss the questions at their own pace.

THE STUDY

INTRODUCTIONS ▼

Art Wars (up to 5 minutes)

Before kids arrive, arrange the chairs in groups of four. In the center of each group of chairs, place a sheet of newsprint, tape, and colored markers. As kids arrive, have them settle into foursomes.

Ask three people in each group to combine their efforts to create a city skyline on the newsprint. Ask the fourth person in each group to work against the other three by trying to change everything they draw into a beautiful mountain scene. After a few minutes, call time and ask groups to display their creations on the walls around the room. Ask:

- **How did you feel trying to draw the city skyline? the mountain scene?**
- **How are those feelings like or unlike the feelings of being a rebel in real life?**

Say: **Lots of adults associate people your age with rebellion. They may point to your attitude, the challenging questions you ask, or even the way you dress as evidence of a rebel spirit. But although most rebellion is negative and harmful, not all rebellion is bad. After all, the Son of God was considered a rebel by almost every leader of his day. And it was accusations of rebellion that led directly to Christ's death on the cross.**

Our goal today is to examine the rebellious aspects of Jesus' character and to see how <u>Jesus is a "holy rebel" you can follow.</u>

INVESTIGATIVE STUDY ▼

God's Chosen Rebel

(30 to 35 minutes)

Say: **To start us off on our rebel quest, let's form four investigative groups that will each examine Jesus' life from a different perspective.**

Once kids are in their four groups, have them all look up these four passages: Luke 6:1-11; 7:36-50; John 2:12-22; and 13:1-9. Then say: **In a moment, I'm going to let you dig into your Bibles to investigate these four different rebellious acts Jesus committed while he was alive on earth. But before you do, let me tell you what I want each group to accomplish in this investigation.**

Give each group one of these four assignments:

- **Group 1**—Create a list titled "Top Ten Reasons Jesus Rebelled"—for example, "Because he wanted to free people from oppression."
- **Group 2**—Choose four modern beliefs or practices that Jesus would rebel against if he were on earth today and decide how he would rebel against them—for example, "Jesus would rebel against racism by building relationships with people from different ethnic backgrounds."
- **Group 3**—Describe five things Jesus might say or do in our class if he started attending our weekly class meetings—for example, "Jesus would wash our feet."
- **Group 4**—Let each group member choose one thing he or she could do as an act of "positive rebellion" in real life—for example, "Tell my friend Trudy about my relationship with Jesus this week."

Say: **Before you begin your investigation, take a moment to pray together in your groups for God to show you what he wants you to learn from these passages. Then as you read the passages, look for any information, examples, or ideas that may help you**

LEADER TIP for God's Chosen Rebel

To help your kids gain a deeper understanding of the passages you assign, photocopy the Depthfinder box titled "Jesus' Rebellious Acts," and distribute copies to each investigative team. Encourage kids to use this information to help them better understand Jesus' actions in each of these situations.

DEPTHFINDER

JESUS' REBELLIOUS ACTS

You may wonder why Jesus acted the way he did in the passages you will explore. Use these background clues to help you interpret these passages correctly:

Luke 6:1-11—The disciples' act of "harvesting" grain on the Sabbath was forbidden by Jewish tradition, as recorded in the Mishna. But Jesus used an example from David's life (1 Samuel 21:1-6) to explain that the Sabbath was established to benefit God's people, not control them.

Luke 7:36-50—Jesus allowed the prostitute to wash his feet with her hair even though he knew it would create a scandal. Christ's concern was not for his own reputation (or that of his host), but for the woman's humble expression of genuine love and gratitude.

John 2:12-22—Worshipers at the temple in Jerusalem were required to present a sacrifice acceptable to a priest and to pay a temple tax. Priests refused to accept foreign currency, so they exchanged travelers' money at expensive rates. They also often rejected any animal that wasn't purchased at the temple. In this way, the priests and merchants made money off of the people's devotion to God's law.

John 13:1-9—In Jesus' day, it was common for the household servant to wash the feet of any visitor who entered. It would be scandalous for a dignified leader to do such a thing—which helps explain Peter's response to Christ's actions (verses 6-8).

For more of Jesus' rebellious acts, check out these passages: Matthew 9:9-12; Mark 7:1-8; Luke 13:10-17; John 5:1-23; John 8:31-59; and John 9:1-11.

accomplish your group's investigative goal.

As each group finishes praying, distribute newsprint and markers. Allow groups no more than twenty minutes to complete their assignments. Offer help to any group having trouble, and be ready to answer questions about Christ's actions in the various passages.

When time is up, have each group present the results of its assignment to the rest of the class. After each group presents its information, ask:

- **What's your reaction to what this group shared?**
- **How does this compare with the rebellious acts we see in ourselves or in our friends?**
- **What's different about Jesus' rebellion?**

After all the groups have presented their information, thank them for their work. Then say: **Now let's explore how our new understanding of Jesus as God's "holy rebel" can inspire you to follow him.**

> **LEADER TIP for The Study**
> Because this topic can be so powerful and relevant to kids' lives, your group members may be tempted to get caught up in issues and lose sight of the deeper biblical principle found in The Point. Help your kids grasp The Point by guiding them to focus on the biblical investigation and by discussing how God's truth connects with reality in their lives.

DEBRIEFING AND COMMITMENT ▼

Jesus and Me

(up to 10 minutes)

Form pairs, and have partners discuss these questions:

- **What did you learn most from this investigation?**
- **What's the main difference between your rebellious actions and Christ's?**

LEADER TIP for Jesus and Me

To streamline the discussion time, write out the discussion questions on newsprint and tape it to the wall. That way kids in each pair can discuss the questions at their own pace.

- **In what ways are your rebellious attitudes similar to Christ's?**
- **What's one positive rebel trait you see in your partner?**
- **Why do you think Jesus rebelled so much during his life on earth?**
- **Based on what you've learned today, how would your rebellion change if you followed Christ's example?**
- **What do you think Christ would do differently in your life if he switched places with you?**
- **What do you think it means for you to be a "rebel for Jesus" in the real world?**
- **Do you think that Jesus is a rebel worth following? Why or why not?**

Have kids break off from their partners and form new groups of three. Ask volunteers to read aloud Matthew 5:10-12 and John 15:18-20. Then have trios discuss these questions:

- **What do these passages tell us about Jesus' attitude toward positive rebellion against the world?**
- **Why do you think Jesus said you are blessed if others persecute you for following him?**
- **Why do you think Jesus warned us that the world would hate us if we followed him?**
- **Based on all we've examined today, why do you think God would want you to be a holy rebel like Jesus?**

"If the world hates you, remember that it hated me first. If you belonged to the world, it would love you as it loves its own. But I have chosen you out of the world, so you don't belong to it. That is why the world hates you. Remember what I told you: A servant is not greater than his master. If people did wrong to me, they will do wrong to you, too. And if they obey my teaching, they will obey yours, too."

John 15:18-20

Holy Rebellion (up to 10 minutes)

Give kids each a pen and one of the "Holy Rebellion" bookmarks you created from the pattern on page 23. Say: **Today we're going to commit an act of positive rebellion that this church won't soon forget. Once we do it, if you decide this Jesus-style rebel life is for you, sign your name on your bookmark and keep it with you as a reminder of your commitment to God.**

Have kids turn to their trio members and respond to these questions:

- **Do you want to follow in Jesus' steps as a holy rebel for God? Why or why not?**
- **What's one thing that would keep you from making a commitment like this to Jesus?**

Have each trio member say a one-sentence prayer for the person on his or her right, asking God to give that person the strength to follow Jesus.

After kids pray, say: **Place your bookmarks in your Bibles for now. Once we plan and execute our positive act of rebellion, you can decide whether you're willing to follow Jesus as a "holy rebel" in your daily life.**

LEADER TIP for Servant Attack

If your church's worship service happens before Sunday school or if you're using this study for a weeknight meeting, alter this final activity by having kids agree to perform their act of positive rebellion during your church's next regular worship service.

PLANNING TIME ▼

Servant Attack (up to 5 minutes)

Give each trio a large bowl and a few towels. Say: **At some point in today's worship service, I'll go up front and read aloud John 13:1-9, which is the story we studied today about Christ's washing the disciples' feet. After I read the passage, I'll ask all the people to take off their shoes and prepare to experience Christ's servant love.**

On my cue, you'll all enter in groups of three and disperse throughout the church to wash people's feet. We won't have time to wash everyone's feet, but each trio should randomly choose to wash at least four people's feet before stopping.

When you're finished, I'll close the experience with a prayer, thanking God for rebelling against our fear and pride and showing

LEADER TIP for Servant Attack

Before this study, make arrangements with your pastor for kids to "invade" the worship service at some point. If your church regularly takes an offering, you might suggest doing the footwashing during that time. Or the experience could take the place of one of your church's worship songs.

DEPTHFINDER — UNDERSTANDING THESE KIDS

Webster defines a rebel as "a person who resists any authority or controls." When kids discuss Jesus as a rebel, they may be tempted to perceive him according to that definition. But Christ's rebellion wasn't against all authority. Rather, he rejected only those authorities that stood in opposition to God's will for his people. Your teenagers should understand that following Jesus doesn't give them the right to rebel against anything they don't like. It only gives them the right to rebel against anything God doesn't like.

us that Jesus is a "holy rebel" we can follow. Then we'll leave through the back door, empty our water basins, and return to the worship service.**

Encourage trios to switch roles each time they wash a new person's feet so everyone gets the chance to do the actual washing. Once kids understand their roles, have them fill their bowls with warm water and wait together outside the worship area until the worship service begins.

handout

Holy Rebellion

Photocopy this bookmark pattern onto card stock so each person can have one.

Buddha and Mohammed—why not?

The Awesome Impact of Jesus' Life on Earth

THE POINT:

God became human for you.

by Stephen Parolini

■ "We're more popular than Jesus now." ■ When John Lennon said this back in 1966, he may have been exaggerating the Beatles' prominence in the world—but he was right about one thing: More people recognize the name Jesus than any other name in history. More than Buddha, more than Mohammed, more than any other religious or military leader. ■ But why? He never led an army, never held an office, never wrote a book, never even traveled much beyond the boundaries of his own country. He seemed to avoid crowds as often as not. And when he did speak, his teachings were so poorly received by the religious leaders that they had him killed. And yet, this man changed the world more than any other can boast. ■ That's because this man did something no other leader has ever done. He rose from the dead. ■ This study compares Jesus with the founders of two other world religions to help teenagers discover the unique ways Jesus' life, death, and resurrection have shaped the world they live in and to help them recognize how his living presence can still impact their lives today.

The Study AT A GLANCE

SECTION	MINUTES	WHAT STUDENTS WILL DO	SUPPLIES
Communication Experience	5 to 10	IN THE FLESH—Attempt to communicate messages from a distance and face to face.	
Comparative Bible Study	25 to 30	LOOKING TO GOD—Explore John 5:19-47 and discuss how Christianity stands out because of its intimate relational connection to God.	Bibles, "Origins of Religions" handouts (pp. 32-33), pencils, paper, index cards, tape
Faith Builder	5 to 10	EVIDENCE OF LIFE—Review Galatians 2:20 and share personal stories that show Jesus is alive today.	Bibles
Group Builder	10 to 15	PERSON TO PERSON—Explore their relationships with one another and spend time in prayer.	

notes:

THE POINT OF *BUDDHA AND MOHAMMED—WHY NOT?*:

God became human for you.

THE BIBLE CONNECTION

JOHN 5:19-47	Jesus explains to the Jews that he is God's Son and has been sent by God.
GALATIANS 2:20	Paul explains that Christ lives in him.

In this study, kids will compare Christianity with two other world religions and will discover how Jesus' life, death, and resurrection can make a personal difference in their lives today.

By comparing Jesus with Mohammed and Buddha, kids can learn what kind of impact Christ had on the world—and what kind of impact he can have in their lives.

Explore the verses in The Bible Connection, then examine the information in the Depthfinder boxes throughout the study to gain a deeper understanding of how these Scriptures connect with your young people.

LEADER TIP for The Study

Because this topic can be so powerful and relevant to kids' lives, your group members may be tempted to get caught up in issues and lose sight of the deeper biblical principle found in The Point. Help your kids grasp The Point by guiding them to focus on the biblical investigation and by discussing how God's truth connects with reality in their lives.

THE STUDY

COMMUNICATION EXPERIENCE ▼

In the Flesh (5 to 10 minutes)

For this experience, gather kids near the door of your meeting room.

Form pairs. Have one person in each pair be the Message Giver and the other be the Message Receiver. Ask the Message Givers to think up an encouraging message they want to give their partners—for example, "I really appreciate your kindness toward others" or "You inspire me with your deep faith." Tell the Message Givers not to tell their partners what the message is yet.

Once the Message Givers have determined what they want to say, send them to another location at least thirty feet from your room. Ask the Message Receivers to remain in the room and close the meeting-room door. Then have the Message Givers attempt to deliver their messages to their partners—all at the same time. Allow kids thirty seconds to try to deliver their messages. Then call everyone together, and have kids find their partners.

Have partners stand face to face and place a hand on each other's shoulder. Then ask the Message Givers to once again communicate their messages.

Afterward, have partners sit and discuss the following questions, sharing insights with the whole group when appropriate:

- **What made it hard to communicate with your partner?**
- **What impact did speaking face to face have on getting the message across?**
- **How is that experience like the impact God had on humanity by sending Jesus to live among us?**

Say: **We don't have to shout or perform to gain God's attention. Because of the work Jesus did on the cross, we can have direct access to and communication with God. Today we're going to explore why God became human for you and compare the impact of his life with other world religions' leaders.**

LEADER TIP for In the Flesh

If other groups are meeting near your kids' room, consider moving this activity near one of the main doors of the building. Then the Message Givers can simply step outside before they try to deliver their messages.

LEADER TIP for The Study

Whenever you ask groups to discuss a list of questions, write the list on newsprint and tape it to a wall so groups can discuss the questions at their own pace.

COMPARATIVE BIBLE STUDY ▼

Looking to God

(25 to 30 minutes)

Form groups of no more than four. Distribute copies of the "Origins of Religions" handout (pp. 32-33) to each group. Have half of the groups read about Buddhism and the other half about

DEPTH FINDER — **UNDERSTANDING THESE KIDS**

Your young people aren't the only ones who've struggled with who Jesus is. In Jesus' day, the Jews also had great difficulty believing Jesus was truly God. Here are a few reasons:

- Although the Jews weren't surprised when Jesus claimed to be a divinely authorized king (Daniel 7:13-14), they were taken aback when he claimed the authority to raise and judge the dead (John 5:20-22). This, according to daily Jewish prayers, was reserved for God alone.
- While the Jews believed God sometimes gave honor to others (Psalm 2:11-12), they had difficulty with what Jesus says in John 5:23, which suggests that Jesus is God.
- The Jews believed that eternal life was supposed to be available only after death, but Jesus promised new life immediately for those who believed and trusted in him (John 5:24-25).

Islam. Groups will also need Bibles, paper, and pencils.

Say: **After you read about your assigned religion, discuss the following questions in your group:**

- **What is most intriguing to you about this religion?**
- **Does this religion encourage an intimate relationship with God and others? Why or why not?**

When each group finishes, have it choose one person to be its Model. Set out index cards and tape. Based on their assigned religions, have group members decorate their Models to illustrate how people should relate to God. For example, kids could demonstrate Islam's focus on "good works" by covering their Models with cards listing various "good deeds." When groups are ready, have them use their Models to teach the rest of the class about their assigned religions.

Applaud each group's efforts. When everyone is finished, have each group read John 5:19-47. Have kids explore these questions in their groups:

- **How is the religion you studied different from Christianity?**
- **Does Christianity encourage an intimate relationship with God and others? Why or why not?**
- **How does that compare to the role of an intimate relationship in Islam? Buddhism?**
- **What does Jesus say in this passage that sets Christianity apart from other religions?**
- **What difference does it make to you that Jesus became human for you?**
- **Why do you think God chose to become human rather than send another prophet?**

After the discussion, have each group choose a new Model. Have the groups decorate their Models as before, only this time using the Models to teach the class how Jesus is different from Mohammed and Buddha.

DEPTH FINDER

UNDERSTANDING THE BIBLE

Through the Scriptures, we get to know Jesus. But we also learn indirectly how early Christians had to defend the truth of Christ's identity against the infiltration of heretical religious views about him.

The Docetics denied that Jesus was fully human and claimed that a man named Simon of Cyrene had been crucified instead of Jesus. The Gospels' frequent reference to Jesus' human qualities—he carried his own cross (John 19:17); he had thirst (John 19:28)—along with the declaration that "the Word became flesh" (John 1:14, NIV) suggests that the Gospel writers were fighting a heresy that was threatening to weaken the truth about Jesus' message of love and salvation.

Gnosticism, which built upon Docetic ideas, appeared in the second century, A.D. The Gnostics believed that the human body was of no value. Therefore, they had no reason to believe in Jesus' physical resurrection. Much like the New Age movement's "higher consciousness" teachings today, Gnosticism was one of the chief threats to the stability of core Christian beliefs.

Paul combated these Gnostic heresies, in part, by pointing Christians back to the truth of Christ's resurrection (1 Corinthians 15:1-11) and the inevitable reality of their own resurrection in Christ (1 Corinthians 15:12-58).

For example, a group could tape a heart shape on its Model to represent Jesus and an empty brain shape to represent Buddha. Again, applaud each group's efforts. When everyone is finished, read aloud Galatians 2:20. Then have kids turn to a partner to answer this question:

- **Why is Paul's statement that Christ lives in him so important in understanding the role of intimate relationship in our Christian faith?**

Say: **The most important difference between Jesus and Buddha or Mohammed is that Jesus rose from the dead. He's still alive today, and he wants a relationship with you. <u>God became human for us</u> so we could know him personally in the "here and now."**

LEADER TIP for Evidence of Life

Because your class may have non-Christian kids in it, be sensitive when asking kids for stories about how Jesus is alive today. Don't require everyone to speak. If appropriate, allow time for kids to ask about what it's like to feel Christ's presence in your life—and let your Christian group members respond before you do.

LEADER TIP for Evidence of Life

When everyone has finished sharing, distribute copies of the "Different World" Depthfinder. Suggest that kids take the sheet home and complete the handout by themselves and then meet with one or two friends to discuss what they've learned. This Depthfinder will help your teenagers gain a deeper understanding of the impact of Jesus' life, death, and resurrection on their world.

FAITH BUILDER ▼

Evidence of Life

(5 to 10 minutes)

Gather everyone together in a circle. Have a volunteer read aloud Galatians 2:20 once again. Then ask volunteers to share

DEPTHFINDER — A DIFFERENT WORLD

How is our world different because of Jesus? Use this self-study to explore some of the unique ways in which Jesus has impacted our world... and to explore how Jesus has impacted your world.

Read the following facts, then jot down how this information impacts you or how it makes you feel:

- Jesus' ministry lasted no more than three years.
- Jesus' original group of followers numbered only about a dozen.
- Jesus didn't have television, radio, or print media to market his message.
- Jesus ended his earthly life crucified on a cross, the way criminals were killed.
- At the end of his ministry, many of Jesus' followers turned against him, betrayed him, or denied him.

Now read the following facts, and note your feelings about them on the back of this page:

- Our calendar is based on Jesus' birth. (B.C. stands for "before Christ" and A.D. stands for "anno Domini," which means "in the year of the Lord.")
- The Bible is the best-selling book in the world.
- Christianity has survived two millennia of arguments, disagreements, and dissension among those who profess it as their religion.
- Miracles still happen today.
- Jesus is the most-recognized figure in history.

How can a man who did so little (compared to other world religions' leaders) impact the world so profoundly? For the answer, read Galatians 2:20. Write your impressions of that verse on the back of this page.

personal stories that show Jesus is alive today. For example, kids might share how Christ has brought new life to a sick relative or how Jesus gave them a new sense of purpose in their own lives. It's OK if only a few kids want to share, but be patient—sometimes it takes a moment or two before someone dares speak first. After a few kids have offered their testimonies, you may wish to share your own, too.

GROUP BUILDER ▼

Person to Person

(10 to 15 minutes)

Say: **One of the ways we can tell that Jesus is alive today is by watching Christians' lives. As Christians, the more time we spend with Jesus the more we become like him. We can each show that Jesus is alive just by letting him live through us. For the next minute, pray silently and ask God to show you how Jesus has lived through you in recent weeks.**

Have kids spend one minute in silent prayer. After the prayer, form pairs, and have kids tell their partners one Christlike quality they see in each other's words and actions. For example, someone might say, "You're always trustworthy" or "I see a great deal of patience in you."

Then have pairs pray together and talk with God about other ways they can let Jesus live through them. Encourage kids to pledge prayer support for their partners throughout the coming week.

handout

ok to copy

ORIGINS OF RELIGIONS

A Brief Look at Islam

ISLAM IS AN ETHNIC RELIGION, rooted in the Arab culture. Its founder, Mohammed, was orphaned soon after birth and reared in poverty.

AT AGE FORTY, after many extended periods of meditation in caves near Mecca, Mohammed felt compelled to proclaim the absolute "oneness" of God and denounce the popular religions of his day.

THOUGH HE NEVER CLAIMED DIVINITY, by A.D. 630, Mohammed was a leader of a new political/religious movement that has since become known as Islam. Those who practice Islam (Muslims) look at Mohammed's writings (collected in a book called the Qur'a-n) as divine revelations.

MOHAMMED DIED IN A.D. 632.

To become a Muslim, one must live out the "five pillars of Islam," which are:

- commit to frequent daily prayers to God.
- commit to periodic fasting.
- go on a pilgrimage to the city of Mecca at least once.
- commit to giving gifts to those in need.
- declare sincerely, "I testify that there is no god but God, and that Mohammed is the Prophet of God."

handout

ok to copy

ORIGINS OF RELIGIONS

A Brief Look at Buddhism

BUDDHISM WAS FOUNDED BY AN INDIAN PRINCE, Siddhartha, the son of a ruler in what is now Nepal. He allegedly lived between 560 and 480 B.C. Tradition says that, at age twenty-nine, he went on a quest to find the answer to the problem of suffering. Six years later, through meditation, he found what he believed was the solution. Siddhartha believed all suffering could be denied by conditioning your mind to reject all human desires that might lead to personal pain. From then on he was known as Buddha, the Enlightened One. He traveled for the next forty-five years, preaching his message to all who would listen, then died at age eighty.

BUDDHISM IS CHARACTERIZED BY MEDITATION designed to aid in the pursuit of Nirvana (the ultimate state of consciousness in which you feel no pain, anxiety, frustration, or despair). There is no absolute deity in Buddhism.

BUDDHISTS LOOK TO THE PA-LI CANON (which contains three sections: the Book of Discipline, the Discourses of Buddha, and the higher subtleties of the law) as their scripture.

The Power of Jesus' Death

HELPING KIDS GRASP THE POWER THEY HAVE THROUGH CHRIST'S DEATH AND RESURRECTION

by Lisa Baba Lauffer

THE POINT:

Jesus died on the cross for you.

Today's young people belong to a generation of do-it-yourselfers. They let themselves into their houses after school. They microwave their own meals. They make their own money, and they buy their own clothes. In many ways, your high school students relish this independence, but when it comes with years of a latchkey existence, it gets old...and lonely.

When you tell today's teenagers that there's Someone who'd do anything for them, many reply with a jaded, "Yeah, right." They're not accustomed to receiving support—they're used to people taking from them. When kids see our country's resources dwindle at their expense, they shrug their shoulders and resign themselves to the loss as one of a host of debts incurred by other generations. Most of today's young people feel powerless to do anything but accept the hand they've been dealt.

That's why the message that Jesus gave his life for them comes as such a surprise. And the idea that they can gain power from his power over sin and death can not only shock them, but can also make them wary. After all, any time anyone has done something on their behalf, it has come with a price tag.

This study will help your students explore how Jesus' death on the cross empowers them to live each day and to live for eternity. Your students can grasp that, though Jesus' death came at a cost to himself, it is a gift of power that comes with no strings attached.

The Study AT A GLANCE

SECTION	MINUTES	WHAT STUDENTS WILL DO	SUPPLIES
Learning Game	15 to 20	POWER PLAY—Play a balloon game in which one team gains more balloons and players as the game progresses.	Red, blue, green, and yellow balloons; newsprint; tape; marker; two empty garbage cans
Active Bible Experience	10 to 15	WHO HAS THE POWER PLAY?—Evaluate the level of power for each person or set of people involved in the Crucifixion.	Bibles, newsprint, tape, balloons, permanent markers
	10 to 15	THE TRUE POWER PLAYER—Explore Scriptures showing that Jesus displayed the truest power through his crucifixion.	Bibles, three-inch nails, adhesive file-folder labels, pens, balloons from previous activity
Response	10 to 15	THE OLD RUGGED CROSS—Create crosses representing Christ's death for them, then individually pray in response to the experience.	Bibles, nails from previous activity, two-inch nails, super glue, twine, scissors

notes:

THE POINT OF *THE POWER OF JESUS' DEATH:*

Jesus died on the cross for you.

THE BIBLE CONNECTION

ISAIAH 53	Isaiah prophesies what Jesus will suffer in exchange for our salvation.
JOHN 18:12-14, 19-24, 33-40; 19:1-24, 28-30; 20:1-18	Jesus dies on the cross and rises from the grave.
ROMANS 5:6-11; 6:5-11	Paul explains that Christ died on the cross for all of us.
MATTHEW 27:51-54; COLOSSIANS 2:13-15; HEBREWS 2:14-15; 1 PETER 3:18-22; 1 JOHN 3:8; REVELATION 1:17-18	These passages describe Jesus' power over sin and death.

In this study, kids will experience an imbalance of power, explore their reactions to that imbalance, then examine the power displayed by different people who were involved in the Crucifixion. They'll also discover that Jesus—though he appeared to be the weakest person in the story—exerted true power, the power that defeated the forces of sin and death.

Through this experience, kids can discover that they have access to Jesus' power in their lives through his death and resurrection—power that gives them ultimate and eternal freedom.

Explore the verses in The Bible Connection, then examine the information in the Depthfinder boxes throughout the study to gain a deeper understanding of how these Scriptures connect with your young people.

LEADER TIP for The Study

Whenever groups discuss a list of questions, write the questions on newsprint, and tape the newsprint to a wall so groups can discuss the questions at their own pace.

BEFORE THE STUDY

On a sheet of newsprint, write the following: "Red=10 points, Blue=20 points, Green=50 points, Yellow=100 points." Tape the newsprint to a wall where everyone will be able to see it. Also bring an equal amount of red, blue, green, and yellow balloons, making sure that you have at least ten of each color or two balloons for each student—whichever amount is greater. (You might want to bring some extras in case balloons pop during the study.)

THE STUDY

LEADER TIP for The Study

Because this topic can be so powerful and relevant to kids' lives, your group members may be tempted to get caught up in issues and may lose sight of the deeper biblical principle found in The Point. Help your kids grasp The Point by guiding them to focus on the biblical investigation and by discussing how God's truth connects with reality in their lives.

LEARNING GAME ▼

Power Play

(15 to 20 minutes)

As students arrive, have them help you inflate all the balloons you brought. Also set the empty garbage cans on opposite sides of the room.

After everyone has arrived and all the balloons are inflated, have kids form two teams, and have teams gather an equal number of each color of balloon. Then say: **Let's start today's study with a game. The object of the game is to get the most points into your opponent's garbage can. As you can see from the list I've posted on the wall, each color of balloon has a different point value: red balloons are worth ten points; blue ones are worth twenty points; greens are worth fifty points; and yellows are worth one hundred. Do what you can to get your balloons into your opponents' goal and to prevent your opponents from getting their balloons into your goal. Be careful not to run over anyone or otherwise hurt someone. We'll play a few rounds, and each round will be two minutes long. Any questions?**

When everyone understands the game, begin. After two minutes, stop the game, and have teams tally their points. Keep tabs on which team is ahead. Then prepare for round two by dividing the balloons between the teams again. This time, give all the red and blue balloons to one team and all the yellow and green balloons to the other team. Ignore any protests the team with the red and blue balloons might have, and begin round two. After two minutes, tally the scores again, add the totals to the round one totals, and announce which team is ahead.

Then prepare for round three. Give the yellow/green team all the yellow, green, *and* blue balloons. Then have half the people from the red team join the now yellow/green/blue team, and begin the game. After two minutes, tally the scores again, and determine which team has the highest score. Then declare the *other* team—the team with the fewest points—the winner.

Have kids form foursomes that include two people from each original team. Have foursomes discuss these questions:

- **What's your reaction to this game?**
- **What were you thinking and feeling as one team got the most valuable balloons? as one team got more people?**
- **What were you thinking and feeling when the team with the fewest points was declared the winner?**
- **What are some other situations in which you've had similar thoughts and feelings? Why?**
- **Have you ever felt that circumstances were stacked against you? If so, when and why? How did you respond?**
- **Have you ever been on a more powerful team than someone**

DEPTHFINDER

UNDERSTANDING THESE KIDS

How do you reach today's young people with the message that they can have eternal life because Jesus died for them? Today's teenagers live in a post-modern world—one that doesn't assume the existence of God or believe in the existence of absolute truth—in which authorities haven't proven themselves trustworthy. With those influences, these young people aren't predisposed to making a onetime, split-second decision to dedicate their lives to God just because an authority lays out a logical argument for doing so. We need to rethink our evangelism strategy when reaching out to today's kids.

In his book *Jesus for a New Generation*, ministry consultant Kevin Graham Ford suggests a new, three-part approach that incorporates the needs of this generation of young people:

Part 1: Embody your beliefs. Live what you believe, and allow Jesus Christ to use you to impact those around you. Today's young people observe Christians, looking for social and emotional changes in Christians' lives to determine whether Christianity is real. Do Christians reach out to homosexuals; the homeless; or unwed, pregnant women? Do Christians love these people with God's love or condemn them? When you attempt to make a real impact in the lives of hurting, needy people, kids in this generation can discover the relevance of Christianity and its message of hope.

Part 2: Approach evangelism as a process. Instead of making a split-second decision to become Christians, many of today's young people will gradually discover and commit to the Gospel's truth. Christians can foster this process by developing genuine, day-to-day relationships with non-Christian young people and sharing with these people the joys and disappointments of their own lives. As non-Christians observe Christ's power impacting day-to-day living, they begin to trust his power for their own lives.

Part 3: Tell the story of Jesus' impact on your life. Stories reach beyond our minds to our hearts and souls, touching the deepest parts of ourselves, parts for which we have no words to explain. Everyone has a story, and we all tell our stories not only in words but in our actions. The Christian can express how Jesus has scripted chapters of his or her life and can invite non-Christians to allow Jesus to impact their stories, too.

We can't draw kids to Christ—only the Holy Spirit can. But as you incorporate these ways of sharing the Gospel with your young people, they'll be more inclined to hearing the Holy Spirit calling them to life in Christ.

else? on a weaker team? If so, when and why? How did you feel?

Say: **Some of you might be familiar with the game of hockey. Often during a hockey game, a player fouls, and the referee sends that player to the penalty box. When this happens, the opposing team has what's called a "power play." They have more players on the ice and therefore have a greater ability to score than the team whose player was penalized.**

A similar thing happened in our balloon game as we progressed through the rounds. And a very similar thing seemed to happen at Jesus' crucifixion. All sorts of people were against him, and those people seemed to have more power than he had. But he turned the tables, and eventually he conquered death's power when <u>he died on the cross for you.</u> Today we're going to explore exactly how he conquered death's power.

ACTIVE BIBLE EXPERIENCE ▼

> **LEADER TIP for Who Has the Power Play?**
>
> You might want to write the Scripture on newsprint for kids to use as a reference in their groups.

Who Has the Power Play? (10 to 15 minutes)

Have kids gather all the balloons used in the previous game and separate the colors. Then have kids form four groups, and give each group a permanent marker and all the balloons of one color. Assign each group one of the following people or groups: Jews, Pilate, Roman soldiers, and Jesus (assign Jesus to the group with the red balloons). Ask:

- **What's your definition of "power"?**

Have all the kids collaborate to create a definition for "power" that they can refer to during the study. Write their definition on newsprint, and post the newsprint where everyone can see it.

Say: **We're going to figure out who held the real power when Jesus Christ died on the cross. In your groups, read the following Scripture: John 18:12-14, 19-24, 33-40; 19:1-24, 28-30.**

Then go through the passage again, and as you do, look for ways that your assigned group or person demonstrated power. Write each way on a separate balloon.

Allow groups five minutes to do this. Set out extra balloons of all colors in case groups need them. After five minutes, have each group set its balloons in front of it and tell the rest of the class the ways its assigned person or group displayed power in the Crucifixion story. When all the groups have shared, have each student turn to a partner to discuss these questions:

- **Who showed the most power up to this point in the Crucifixion story? Explain.**
- **How did Jesus' power compare to the power of his accusers and executioners?**
- **How was the power imbalance in our balloon game like the power imbalance in the Crucifixion story? How was it different?**
- **At this point in the story, would you rather be on the team of the Jews, Pilate, and the Roman soldiers or on Jesus' team? Explain.**

Invite pairs to share their answers to the above questions. Then say:

POINT **At this point in the story, things looked pretty bleak for Jesus. But Jesus died on the cross for you, and his death was not in vain.**

Have kids gather the balloons in one corner of the room for later use.

> **LEADER TIP for The True Power Player**
>
> If you don't have three-inch nails, have kids place the tags on straight pins and then use the pins to pop the balloons.

The True Power Player (10 to 15 minutes)

Say: **Let's look at the end of Jesus' crucifixion story and some other Scripture passages to discover who held the real power in this situation.**

Have kids form three groups, and assign each group one of the following sets of Bible passages:

- John 20:1-18;
- Matthew 27:51-54; Colossians 2:13-15; and Hebrews 2:14-15; and
- 1 Peter 3:18-22; 1 John 3:8; and Revelation 1:17-18.

Give each student a three-inch nail, and give each group some adhesive file-folder labels and pens to share. Say: **In your group, read the Scripture I've assigned to you. As you do, look for the ways Jesus**

displayed power through his death on the cross. Write each way on one of the file-folder labels I gave you, and peel the label off the backing. Place a nail in the middle of the sticky side of the label, then bring the ends of the label together to stick the label to itself over the nail so the nail has a tag. Make a nail with a tag for each display of Jesus' power you find in your Bible passages. Make sure you have enough tagged nails for each person in your group to have one. You may repeat ways Jesus showed power in order to create a nail for each group member.

Allow groups five minutes to create their tagged nails. As they do, separate the balloons the kids created in the previous activity, placing the balloons representing the Jews, Pilate, and the Roman soldiers in one pile.

After groups finish, have each group tell the rest of the class the ways Jesus displayed power through his death on the cross and his resurrection. Then say: **<u>When Jesus died on the cross for you and me,</u> he did the most powerful thing he could have done: He conquered all the power of sin and death. To symbolize**

DEPTHFINDER — UNDERSTANDING THE BIBLE

What did Jesus do between his death on the cross and his resurrection? Did he lay as a corpse in his tomb? Or was he busy doing his Father's work?

First Peter 3:18-20 gives us a clue, and yet this passage's meaning is obscure. What does it mean that "in the spirit he went and preached to the spirits in prison who refused to obey God long ago in the time of Noah"? *The Life Application Bible: New Testament* presents three possible interpretations:

1. Between his death and resurrection, Christ proclaimed salvation to the people who faithfully followed God in Old Testament times;
2. With Christ's spirit within him, Noah preached to souls of the dead imprisoned by sin; and
3. Jesus Christ, between his death and resurrection, went to Hades to announce his victory over sin and death to the souls that had resided there since Noah's day.

Whichever interpretation one adopts, Jesus Christ was busy between his death and resurrection. He exercised his power over death, power that we can rely on to conquer death and grant us eternal life.

LEADER TIP for The True Power Player

When you ask the last discussion question, be prepared for a variety of responses. Some of your students who already have a relationship with Jesus may make new commitments to follow him more closely. Others who haven't yet made this decision may wish to do so now. Invite these students to talk with you after class to discuss any questions they have and, if they wish, pray with you to begin a new life with Jesus Christ. Still others may not be ready to make any response to Jesus based on this study. That's OK. Remember that you're planting seeds that may someday grow into a full-fledged relationship with Jesus Christ.

this, take the nails you've just created, and pop all the balloons except the red ones you made in the last activity.

After students have finished, have them form foursomes that include one person from each group in the previous activity (Jews, Pilate, Roman soldiers, and Jesus). Have foursomes discuss these questions:

- **What were you thinking and feeling as you popped the balloons?**
- **How was popping the balloons with the nails like how Jesus conquered the power of sin and death by dying on the cross?**
- **What's your reaction to Jesus' dying on the cross for you? to what his death accomplished for you?**
- **Would you like to respond in any way to what Jesus has done for you? If so, how?**

Invite students to express to the class their answers to any of the questions above. Then say: **When the Jews, Pilate, and the Roman soldiers worked together to crucify Jesus, it looked like it was all over for Jesus and for those who cared about him. But his death was only the beginning. His death conquered the power of sin and death. And because Jesus died on the cross for you and for me, we can access that power over sin and death every day of our lives.**

RESPONSE ▼

The Old Rugged Cross

(10 to 15 minutes)

Set out one two-inch nail for each student, super glue, twine, and scissors. Have each student keep his or her three-inch nail from the previous activity and gather a two-inch nail and a yard of twine. Have students create a cross with their two-inch and three-inch nails, super-gluing them together where they meet. (They may choose whether or not they'd like to peel the tag from their three-inch nails.) Then have each student tie his or her twine around the head of the three-inch nail and tie the loose ends of the twine together, making a rugged cross necklace.

LEADER TIP for The Old Rugged Cross

To help kids remember the passages during this time of solitude, write the passages on a sheet of newsprint, and post the newsprint where everyone can see it.

DEPTH FINDER

UNDERSTANDING THESE KIDS

Why would a message of Jesus' power appeal to your young people? Because they're growing up in a context that generally leaves them feeling powerless. Here are a few quotes that express why your students feel this way and how they express it:

"Gone for many are key support systems that in the past were important to child-rearing and a young person's sense of security: strong families (torn apart today by the epidemic of divorce and other forces); friendly and supportive neighborhoods; and a society generally in agreement on vital core values. It is little wonder that many adults today are glad they are not growing up in today's world."

—George H. Gallup, *Scared: Growing Up in America*

"Yet while many of us are grateful to live in America, we recognize and worry about the fact that our future has been sold out—put up for sale to the highest special-interest bidder.

"Our political leaders have run up tremendous debts—economic, social, and environmental burdens that our generation and generations to come must confront. Now, on the edge of a new millennium, our generation has the difficult task of beginning the great American cleanup."

—Rob Nelson and Jon Cowan, *Revolution X: A Survival Guide for Our Generation*

"I know that for those now in junior high and high school in America's cities, the fear of gang violence and drive-by shootings adds to stress even for those young people whose families are healthy. Fistfights have been replaced by gang fights with lethal weapons...

"Those with no personal experience of such traumatic events are nevertheless aware that this is the way life really is for their contemporaries—and thus for themselves. They live with the very realistic expectation that something bad will probably happen to them. They know that life is hostile and dangerous."

—William Mahedy and Janet Bernardi, *A Generation Alone*

"My generation is an emotional basket case. As a class, our self-esteem is low. The prevalence of body art (tattoos) on both young men and young women suggests a lack of self-respect and self-esteem... the body is no longer a temple. It is just another bare wall upon which to scrawl our graffiti."

—Kevin Graham Ford, *Jesus for a New Generation*

While today's young people may *feel* powerless, they truly aren't. They have access to the greatest power available—Jesus' power over sin and death. Help your students grasp this reality through this study and through your interactions with them. When kids understand that they have Jesus' death-defying, life-giving power behind them, they can face today's circumstances with hope and joy—enough hope and joy to share with those around them and to make a difference in their world.

While today's young people may feel powerless, they truly aren't. They have access to the greatest power available—Jesus' power over sin and death.

Say: **This cross is a symbol of what Jesus Christ did when <u>he died on the cross for you.</u> Find a place in this room where you can spend some private time with God. Bring a Bible and your cross with you.**

When kids are settled, say: **Today you've discovered how, when everything looked hopeless, Jesus had the power to conquer sin and death. Now, as you spend some time in solitude, read one or all of the following passages: Isaiah 53; Romans 5:6-11; and Romans 6:5-11. As you read one or all of these passages, look for how Christ's death on the cross and resurrection impacted *you.* Then spend some time in prayer responding to what you discover.**

Allow kids five minutes to read and pray. Then have kids find partners and share with their partners any decisions they made or insights they had as they read and prayed.

"But he took our **suffering** on him
and felt our **pain** for us.
We saw his **suffering**
and thought God was **PUNISHING** him.
But he was wounded for the wrong we did;
he was **crushed** for the evil we did.
The **PUNISHMENT**, which made us well,
was given to him,
and we are **healed** because of his wounds.
We all have w a n d e r e d away like sheep;
each of us has g o n e his own way.
But the Lord has put on him the **PUNISHMENT**
for all the evil we have done."

Isaiah 53:4-6

Before dismissing the class, have students complete this sentence to their partners: "I'm glad that Jesus died on the cross for you because..." Encourage kids to take their crosses home as reminders of Christ's death for them and of his power. Tell kids to hang their crosses where they'll see them, such as on doorknobs or bedposts.

NOBLE birth

HELPING KIDS FIND THEIR IDENTITY IN JESUS

by Karl Leuthauser

THE POINT:

Jesus is with you, and he understands.

■ Society screams the sermon of false significance to your kids. Television, movies, and magazines preach that importance is measured by possessions, popularity, and appearance. Friends reinforce the message. ■ Your kids endeavor to find a sense of self in the offerings of society only to find deeper hunger. As long as young people believe the message that they're insignificant, false foundations of image will entice them with irresistible strength. ■ Fortunately, there's hope for your kids. It's not found by realizing the potential of personal power. It's not offered in the mantras of self-esteem. It's found in our true identity as beloved children of the Creator of the universe. ■ This study will help your kids grasp how Jesus Christ, the giver of true identity, stands by them when everything else they lean on for self-worth crumbles at their feet.

The Study AT A GLANCE

SECTION	MINUTES	WHAT STUDENTS WILL DO	SUPPLIES
Emotional Connection	15 to 20	SYMBOLIC SUPPLIES—Use office supplies to illustrate their self-image and Jesus' identity.	Bibles, various office supplies
Creative Bible Experience	20 to 25	FALSE IMAGES—Make self-image collages on a variety of "canvases" and see which one resists the "rip test."	Bibles, magazines and newspapers, glue, red construction paper, a photocopy of the "Greenback" handout (p. 55), an old Bible, a sheet of tinfoil, scissors, index cards, pen, tape
	5 to 10	SELF-ASSURANCE—Use pieces of their collages to express their identification with Christ.	Bibles, tape, collages from the previous activity
Personal Application	5 to 10	IN HIS IMAGE—Trace one another's silhouettes and write their identity in Jesus within the tracings.	Bibles, markers, newsprint

notes:

THE POINT OF ***NOBLE BIRTH:***

Jesus is with you, and he understands.

THE BIBLE CONNECTION

1 SAMUEL 16:7; LUKE 9:46-48; 16:13	God gives us his perspective on areas in which people place their identity.
PSALM 146:5-11; MATTHEW 6:19-21	God shows us where to put our hope and identity.
ISAIAH 53:1-9	Isaiah predicts that Jesus will be rejected by the people of his day.
JOHN 5:19; 8:28; 8:54; 12:49-50; 14:10-11	Jesus finds his direction and purpose in the Father.
JOHN 15:1-8	Jesus tells us that we need to remain in him.

In this study, kids will examine various foundations of self-image and will evaluate the reliability of each one. Then kids will look at their identity in Christ and will brainstorm about ways to express it.

Through this experience, kids can recognize that even when their earthly foundations of self-image crumble, Jesus is with them and understands their thoughts and feelings. Kids can also realize that they can find their identity in their relationship with Jesus Christ, the only unshakable refuge for definition of self-image.

Explore the verses in The Bible Connection, then examine the information in the Depthfinder boxes throughout the study to gain a deeper understanding of how these Scriptures connect with your young people.

BEFORE THE STUDY

Gather two office supplies for every student—a stapler, a pen, tape, a book, a tack, a spoon, paper, or a computer disk, for example. This activity depends so much on the creativity of the kids that almost anything will do. Place the items in piles of eight around the room. Make sure each pile has eight distinct items.

Make one photocopy of the "Greenback" handout (p. 55) on green paper, and cut it out. Using the red construction paper, cut out a heart the size of a piece of notebook paper. Find an old Bible that could use a permanent, creative cover.

LEADER TIP for The Study

Whenever groups discuss a list of questions, write the list on newsprint and tape it to a wall so groups can discuss the questions at their own pace.

THE STUDY

EMOTIONAL CONNECTION ▼

Symbolic Supplies (15 to 20 minutes)

As the kids arrive, have them form groups of four around the piles of office supplies. Say: **I want you to tell the people in your group who you are by using the items you see in front of you. Pick one or two of the items that represent who you are in some way, then tell the group why you chose those items. After you're done, put the items back in the pile so each group member can use all the items for his or her turn.**

After they finish, have the group members number off from one to four. Assign John 5:19 to the "ones," John 8:28 to the "twos," John 8:54 to the "threes," and John 12:49-50 to the "fours." Ask each group member to read the passage to his or her group. Then tell the groups to pick two items from their piles that Jesus might use to describe his identity. Have each group choose a representative to share with the whole class the items they chose and how they represent Jesus' identity. Allow each representative a turn to share, then ask:

- **How well did the objects reflect your whole identity? Jesus' identity? Why?**
- **How was comparing your identity to the supplies like basing your self-worth on appearance, money, or popularity? How was it different?**

Ask a volunteer to read John 14:10-11. Ask:

- **Why do you think Jesus looked to the Father for his direction and purpose?**

LEADER TIP for Symbolic Supplies

The items you use for this activity do not need to be unique to each group. It may save preparation time to use items that you have in abundance. For example, you might want to grab one paper clip and one pen for each group. If you do this, make certain that you don't give two of the same item to a group.

DEPTHFINDER — UNDERSTANDING THESE KIDS

In a survey of more than 46,000 teenagers, Dr. Peter Benson, president of the Search Institute in Minneapolis, found that 53 percent had never spent time during the last year helping people who are poor, hungry, or sick. Yet according to Dr. Benson, "Students who engage in helping behavior on a weekly basis are... less likely than non-helpers to report risky behaviors" (The Troubled Journey: A Profile of American Youth brochure).

Serving others helps kids develop a healthy sense of self-image. When kids see that others face difficulties, they can put their own problems in proper perspective. Young people also gain a sense of purpose when they serve others. Having a positive affect on others enables kids to see their value as helpful and needed individuals.

God has given us all abilities and talents that we can share with others (Ephesians 4:7,11-12). Doing so changes the lives of the receiver and the giver. Obeying God's call to serve helps us remember who we are and powerfully shapes our self-image.

● **What can we learn from his example?**

Ask a volunteer to read John 15:1-8. Then say: **Jesus wants us to know that we can't do anything without him. He gave us an example by depending on the Father for everything he did. Jesus wants us to find our direction and purpose in him so our lives are fruitful and worthwhile. When you aren't sure of who you are or what you stand for, remember that <u>Jesus is with you, and he understands.</u>**

Have groups form circles around the items. Have each group member choose an item from the pile that symbolizes how he or she sees Jesus in the person to his or her left. Then have each student explain to his or her group why he or she chose that item.

CREATIVE BIBLE EXPERIENCE ▼

False Images

(20 to 25 minutes)

Have students form four groups. Then say: **Sometimes we forget who we are, and we evaluate our self-worth by things other than Jesus. Let's take some time to look at the false things we use to evaluate our self-worth. To start, discuss the following questions with your group:**

● **Have you ever evaluated your self-worth by something that wasn't worthwhile? If so, what?**

● **What are some other things people use to evaluate their self-worth?**

After groups have finished, say: **We're going to look at a few ways people measure their personal value. To help us do this, I'd like you to make collages that describe the perspectives of certain types of people.**

Distribute the old Bible, the photocopied Greenback, the construction paper heart, and the tinfoil between the groups. Tell the kids that you want them to use the items as the "canvases" for their collages. Place the magazines, newspapers, scissors, and glue in the middle of the room. Tell the kids to use pictures, words, and graphics from the magazines and newspapers as symbols for their collages.

Then say: **The group with the heart should make a collage representing the perspective of a person who is very popular. The group with the Greenback should make a collage representing the perspective of a rich person. The group with the tinfoil should make a collage representing the perspective of a person who is very attractive. The group with the Bible should, on the cover of the Bible, make a collage representing the perspective of a person who has a relationship with Jesus.**

As the students work on their collages, write "Gossip," "Expectations," "Bankruptcy," "Theft," "Time," "Accidents," "Difficulties," and "Troubles" on eight separate index cards. Distribute the cards randomly to eight kids, and ask each to tape the card to the front of his or her shirt. After the groups have finished the collages, have them come together and put the

LEADER TIP for False Images

If you don't want to permanently change the cover of a Bible, have the kids use clear tape to stick the symbols to the Bible. You may want to test this before the study to make certain it won't ruin the cover.

① What are little children like? (10 adjectives)

> **LEADER TIP for The Study**
>
> Because this topic can be so powerful and relevant to kids' lives, your group members may be tempted to get caught up in issues and may lose sight of the deeper biblical principle found in The Point. Help your kids grasp The Point by guiding them to focus on the biblical investigation and by discussing how God's truth connects with reality in their lives.

collages in the middle of the gro
lage on the heart. Ask:

● **How is this collage like a**
your own identity? How is it

● **What's important to a po**

● **Is popularity a good or a**

Have a volunteer read aloud

● **What do these verses say**
our popularity?

Have the students look at the

● **Do you see anything on t**
collage that symbolizes who y

● **How would your life be d**
dollars?

● **How important is money to you? Why?**

Have a volunteer read Luke 16:13. Then ask:

● **What does this verse say about evaluating ourselves by how much money we have?**

Instruct the teenagers to look at the collage on the tinfoil. Then ask:

● **What similarities do you see between this collage and a collage you might make to represent your identity? What differences do you see?**

● **Are attractive people treated better than unattractive people are? If so, why?**

● **Is it important to be attractive?**

Have a volunteer read aloud 1 Samuel 16:7. Ask:

● **What does this verse say about evaluating ourselves by the way we look?**

Then say: **No matter how you evaluate your self-worth, the world will try to rip you apart. If you evaluate yourself by your popularity, gossip and expectations may come against you.** Have the teenagers wearing the "Gossip" and "Expectations" index cards each hold a side of the collage on the heart. Tell the group that the two students stand for gossip and expectations. Then say: **If you evaluate yourself by your money, bankruptcy or theft may steal your foundation.** Have students wearing the "Bankruptcy" and "Theft" index cards each hold a side of the collage on the Greenback. Tell the group that the two kids symbolize bankruptcy and theft. Say: **It's dangerous to base your identity on your looks because time or accidents can take outward beauty away.** Ask the kids wearing the "Time" and "Accidents" index cards each to hold a side of the collage on tinfoil. Tell the group that the two kids symbolize time and accidents. Say: **Watch what happens when these forces come against false foundations of self-image.** Instruct the people holding the collages to pull them apart so they rip. Have the kids rip the collages to many pieces. Instruct the kids to put the pieces into a pile in the center of the group. Then ask volunteers to read aloud Matthew 6:19-21 and Psalm 146:5-11. Ask:

● **According to these verses, on what should we base our identity? Why?**

Instruct the students wearing the "Difficulties" and "Troubles" index cards each to hold a side of the collage on the cover of the Bible. Explain

DEPTHFINDER

UNDERSTANDING THESE KIDS

One way to help kids improve their self-image is to give them opportunities to be actively involved in their youth group. To do this you could recruit kids to set up before meetings and clean up afterward, ask kids to help with worship, ask volunteers to make contacts for fun-nights and servant events, ask volunteers to coordinate snacks, provide opportunities for kids to teach or share, or ask kids to be prayer partners with others.

If you choose to offer kids one or more of these opportunities, make certain you give the kids ample support for the activities they choose. Thank and praise them for their efforts even if you end up doing more work than you originally planned. Don't underestimate your kids' abilities to serve. You may be surprised at the effort they demonstrate when they feel that they provide an important service.

that these kids stand for difficulties and troubles. Ask the two kids to try to pull the Bible apart. Then say: **The only safe foundation on which to base your identity is God. No matter what the foundation of your self-image is, troubles and difficulties will come to tear you into two. Popularity, money, good looks, and other earthly foundations may be torn apart or destroyed, but God is unshakable. When troubles and difficulties come, remember that Jesus is with you, and he understands. If you base your identity on your relationship with him, you will never be ripped apart.**

Self-Assurance (5 to 10 minutes)

Ask the students to look for one symbol they can identify with in the pile of collages that have been ripped up. For example, if a teenager is interested in sports, he or she can find a picture of a ball or a tennis shoe. Encourage every person to find one symbol. If someone can't find a symbol, have that person take a piece of a collage that he or she finds interesting. Have kids form groups of three, and instruct the group members to take their collage pieces with them. Ask the groups to read Isaiah 53:1-9 and discuss the following questions.

- **Who are these verses talking about?**
- **According to these verses, how did people treat Jesus?**
- **What was Jesus' outward appearance like?**
- **How would you feel about yourself if these verses described you? Why?**
- **Do you find any comfort in these verses? If so, what?**

Then say: **Jesus wasn't rich, he wasn't good-looking, and he wasn't popular. He went through incredible humiliation and mockery. When you feel worthless or unwanted, remember that Jesus has gone through the worst kind of rejection. When you feel that your foundation has been ripped apart, know that Jesus is with you, and he understands everything you're going through. You can base your identity on him and know that it will be safe.**

Have each student take his or her collage piece and stick a piece of rolled tape to it. Ask the kids to tape their pieces to the collage on the

Bible. As they tape their pieces to the Bible, remind kids that Jesus can pick up the pieces of shattered images and that he is the only safe foundation for their identity.

PERSONAL APPLICATION ▼

In His Image

(5 to 10 minutes)

Have the kids get into pairs. Give each student a large sheet of newsprint, and put the markers in the middle of the room. Say: **We've looked at some ways people measure their self-worth. Now let's look at the unshakable and true image we have in Jesus. To do this, I'd like your partner to trace your silhouette on the sheet of newsprint I've given you.**

After kids finish tracing, have each pair come up with three things that describe their identity in Jesus from each of the following passages: John 15:9-17; Romans 6:1-7; and Romans 8:9-17. Have the kids write on their silhouettes the attributes of their identity that they discovered in the Bible passages. For example, they may want to write "Child of God" after reading Romans 8:9-17. When they finish, say: **Look at the words you've written on the silhouette. God says that you possess these qualities regardless of how you feel. In your pairs, take some time to pray for each other. If you have difficulty believing or acting according to your identity in Christ, ask God for help. If you feel that you have a hold on your identity in Jesus, give a prayer of praise for who he's made you.**

After kids finish, say: **Take your silhouettes home with you as a reminder of your identity in Jesus. When you feel that you aren't good enough or if you feel that your world is caving in, look at your silhouette, and hold fast to who you are. Remember that <u>Jesus is with you, and he understands.</u>**

LEADER TIP for In His Image

If you don't have enough newsprint for everyone to trace their partners' entire bodies, have them trace their partners' bodies from the waist up or from the neck up.

DEPTH FINDER — UNDERSTANDING THESE KIDS

"There is nothing at all wrong with self-esteem, but it has to be linked to an achievement... Just memorizing the phrase 'I'm great' doesn't convince anyone."

—William Damon, child development expert (Nanci Hellmich, "Emphasizing achievement, not faint praise," USA Today, Oct. 24, 1995)

Helping kids with their self-image is a long and difficult process. Giving them the opportunity to know who they are in Christ is the first step. Your young people have incredible value and worth because they're God's children. Many kids can't believe this because they're actively devalued by important people in their lives.

To help kids grasp their worth in Jesus, try to catch them acting like a child of God. Give them opportunities to grow, then notice their growth. Offer sincere praise for small and large accomplishments. Your input and opinions matter to the kids. You have the opportunity to help them believe their true identity by giving generous and sincere encouragement.

handout

"GreenBAcK"

helpful stuff

why Active and Interactive Learning works with teenagers

Let's Start With the Big Picture

Think back to a major life lesson you've learned.

Got it? Now answer these questions:

- Did you learn your lesson from something you read?
- Did you learn it from something you heard?
- Did you learn it from something you experienced?

If you're like 99 percent of your peers, you answered "yes" only to the third question—you learned your life lesson from something you experienced.

This simple test illustrates the most convincing reason for using active and interactive learning with young people: People learn best through experience. Or to put it even more simply, people learn by doing.

Learning by doing is what active learning is all about. No more sitting quietly in chairs and listening to a speaker expound theories about God—that's passive learning. Active learning gets kids out of their chairs and into the experience of life. With active learning, kids get to *do* what they're studying. They *feel* the effects of the principles you teach. They *learn* by experiencing truth firsthand.

Active learning works because it recognizes three basic learning needs and uses them in concert to enable young people to make discoveries on their own and to find practical life applications for the truths they believe.

So what are these three basic learning needs?

1. Teenagers need action.
2. Teenagers need to think.
3. Teenagers need to talk.

Read on to find out exactly how these needs will be met by using the active and interactive learning techniques in Group's Core Belief Bible Study Series in your youth group.

1. Teenagers Need Action

Aircraft pilots know well the difference between passive and active learning. Their passive learning comes through listening to flight instructors and reading flight-instruction books. Their active learning comes through actually flying an airplane or flight simulator. Books and lectures may be helpful, but pilots really learn to fly by manipulating a plane's controls themselves.

We can help young people learn in a similar way. Though we may engage students passively in some reading and listening to teachers, their understanding and application of God's Word will really take off through simulated and real-life experiences.

Forms of active learning include simulation games; role-plays; service projects; experiments; research projects; group pantomimes; mock trials; construction projects; purposeful games; field trips; and, of course, the most powerful form of active learning—real-life experiences.

We can more fully explain active learning by exploring four of its characteristics:

- **Active learning is an adventure.** Passive learning is almost always predictable. Students sit passively while the teacher or speaker follows a planned outline or script.

In active learning, kids may learn lessons the teacher never envisioned. Because the leader trusts students to help create the learning experience, learners may venture into unforeseen discoveries. And often the teacher learns as much as the students.

- **Active learning is fun and captivating.** What are we communicating when we say, "OK, the fun's over—time to talk about God"? What's the hidden message? That joy is separate from God? And that learning is separate from joy?

What a shame.

Active learning is not joyless. One seventh-grader we interviewed clearly remembered her best Sunday school lesson: "Jesus was the light, and we went into a dark room and shut off the lights. We had a candle, and we learned that Jesus is the light and the dark can't shut off the light." That's active learning. Deena enjoyed the lesson. She had fun. And she learned.

Active learning intrigues people. Whether they find a foot-washing experience captivating or maybe a bit uncomfortable, they learn. And they learn on a level deeper than any work sheet or teacher's lecture could ever reach.

- **Active learning involves everyone.** Here the difference between passive and active learning becomes abundantly clear. It's like the difference between watching a football game on television and actually playing in the game.

The "trust walk" provides a good example of involving everyone in active learning. Half of the group members put on blindfolds; the other half serve as guides. The "blind" people trust the guides to lead them through the building or outdoors. The guides prevent the blind people from falling down stairs or tripping over rocks. Everyone needs to participate to learn the inherent lessons of trust, faith, doubt, fear, confidence, and servanthood. Passive spectators of this experience would learn little, but participants learn a great deal.

- **Active learning is focused through debriefing.** Activity simply for activity's sake doesn't usually result in good learning. Debriefing—evaluating an experience by discussing it in pairs or small groups—helps focus the experience and draw out its meaning. Debriefing helps sort and order the information students gather during the experience. It helps learners relate the recently experienced activity to their lives.

The process of debriefing is best started immediately after an experience. We use a three-step process in debriefing: reflection, interpretation, and application.

Reflection—This first step asks the students, "How did you feel?" Active-learning experiences typically evoke an emotional reaction, so it's appropriate to begin debriefing at that level.

Some people ask, "What do feelings have to do with education?" Feelings have everything to do with education. Think back again to that time in your life when you learned a big lesson. In all likelihood, strong feelings accompanied that lesson. Our emotions tend to cement things into our memories.

When you're debriefing, use open-ended questions to probe feelings. Avoid questions that can be answered with a "yes" or "no." Let your learners know that there are no wrong answers to these "feeling" questions. Everyone's feelings are valid.

Interpretation—The next step in the debriefing process asks, "What does this mean to you? How is this experience like or unlike some other aspect of your life?" Now you're asking people to identify a message or principle from the experience.

You want your learners to discover the message for themselves. So instead of telling students your answers, take the time to ask questions that encourage self-discovery. Use Scripture and discussion in pairs or small groups to explore how the actions and effects of the activity might translate to their lives.

Alert! Some of your people may interpret wonderful messages that you never intended. That's not failure! That's the Holy Spirit at work. God allows us to catch different glimpses of his kingdom even when we all look through the same glass.

Application—The final debriefing step asks, "What will you do about it?" This step moves learning into action. Your young people have shared a common experience. They've discovered a principle. Now they must create something new with what they've just experienced and interpreted. They must integrate the message into their lives.

The application stage of debriefing calls for a decision. Ask your students how they'll change, how they'll grow, what they'll do as a result of your time together.

2. Teenagers Need to Think

Today's students have been trained not to think. They aren't dumber than previous generations. We've simply conditioned them not to use their heads.

You see, we've trained our kids to respond with the simplistic answers they think the teacher wants to hear. Fill-in-the-blank student workbooks and teachers who ask dead-end questions such as "What's the capital of Delaware?" have produced kids and adults who have learned not to think.

And it doesn't just happen in junior high or high school. Our children are schooled very early not to think. Teachers attempt to help kids read with nonsensical fill-in-the-blank drills, word scrambles, and missing-letter puzzles.

Helping teenagers think requires a paradigm shift in how we teach. We need to plan for and set aside time for higher-order thinking and be willing to reduce our time spent on lower-order parroting. Group's Core Belief Bible Study Series is designed to help you do just that.

Thinking classrooms look quite different from traditional classrooms. In most church environments, the teacher does most of the talking and hopes that knowledge will transmit from his or her brain to the students'. In thinking settings, the teacher coaches students to ponder, wonder, imagine, and problem-solve.

3. Teenagers Need to Talk

Everyone knows that the person who learns the most in any class is the teacher. Explaining a concept to someone else is usually more helpful to the explainer than to the listener. So why not let the students do more teaching? That's one of the chief benefits of letting kids do the talking. This process is called interactive learning.

What is interactive learning? Interactive learning occurs when students discuss and work cooperatively in pairs or small groups.

Interactive learning encourages learners to work together. It honors the fact that students can learn from one another, not just from the teacher. Students work together in pairs or small groups to accomplish shared goals. They build together, discuss together, and present together. They teach each other and learn from one another. Success as a group is celebrated. Positive interdependence promotes individual and group learning.

Interactive learning not only helps people learn but also helps learners feel better about themselves and get along better with others. It accomplishes these things more effectively than the independent or competitive methods.

Here's a selection of interactive learning techniques that are used in Group's Core Belief Bible Study Series. With any of these models, leaders may assign students to specific partners or small groups. This will maximize cooperation and learning by preventing all the "rowdies" from linking up. And it will allow for new friendships to form outside of established cliques.

Following any period of partner or small-group work, the leader may reconvene the entire class for large-group processing. During this time the teacher may ask for reports or discoveries from individuals or teams. This technique builds in accountability for the teacherless pairs and small groups.

Pair-Share—With this technique each student turns to a partner and responds to a question or problem from the teacher or leader. Every learner responds. There are no passive observers. The teacher may then ask people to share their partners' responses.

Study Partners—Most curricula and most teachers call for Scripture passages to be read to the whole class by one person. One reads; the others doze.

Why not relinquish some teacher control and let partners read and react with each other? They'll all be involved—and will learn more.

Learning Groups—Students work together in small groups to create a model, design artwork, or study a passage or story; then they discuss what they learned through the experience. Each person in the learning group may be assigned a specific role. Here are some examples:

Reader

Recorder (makes notes of key thoughts expressed during the reading or discussion)

Checker (makes sure everyone understands and agrees with answers arrived at by the group)

Encourager (urges silent members to share their thoughts)

When everyone has a specific responsibility, knows what it is, and contributes to a small group, much is accomplished and much is learned.

Summary Partners—One student reads a paragraph, then the partner summarizes the paragraph or interprets its meaning. Partners alternate roles with each paragraph.

The paraphrasing technique also works well in discussions. Anyone who wishes to share a thought must first paraphrase what the previous person said. This sharpens listening skills and demonstrates the power of feedback communication.

Jigsaw—Each person in a small group examines a different concept, Scripture, or part of an issue. Then each teaches the others in the group. Thus, all members teach, and all must learn the others' discoveries. This technique is called a jigsaw because individuals are responsible to their group for different pieces of the puzzle.

JIGSAW EXAMPLE

Here's an example of a jigsaw.

Assign four-person teams. Have teammates each number off from one to four. Have all the Ones go to one corner of the room, all the Twos to another corner, and so on.

Tell team members they're responsible for learning information in their numbered corners and then for teaching their team members when they return to their original teams.

Give the following assignments to various groups:

Ones: Read Psalm 22. Discuss and list the prophecies made about Jesus.

Twos: Read Isaiah 52:13–53:12. Discuss and list the prophecies made about Jesus.

Threes: Read Matthew 27:1-32. Discuss and list the things that happened to Jesus.

Fours: Read Matthew 27:33-66. Discuss and list the things that happened to Jesus.

After the corner groups meet and discuss, instruct all learners to return to their original teams and report what they've learned. Then have each team determine which prophecies about Jesus were fulfilled in the passages from Matthew.

Call on various individuals in each team to report one or two prophecies that were fulfilled.

You Can Do It Too!

All this information may sound revolutionary to you, but it's really not. God has been using active and interactive learning to teach his people for generations. Just look at Abraham and Isaac, Jacob and Esau, Moses and the Israelites, Ruth and Boaz. And then there's Jesus, who used active learning all the time!

Group's Core Belief Bible Study Series makes it easy for you to use active and interactive learning with your group. The active and interactive elements are automatically built in! Just follow the outlines, and watch as your kids grow through experience and positive interaction with others.

FOR DEEPER STUDY

For more information on incorporating active and interactive learning into your work with teenagers, check out these resources:

- *Why Nobody Learns Much of Anything at Church: And How to Fix It,* by Thom and Joani Schultz (Group Publishing) and
- *Do It! Active Learning in Youth Ministry,* by Thom and Joani Schultz (Group Publishing).

your evaluation of core belief

Bible Study Series
for senior high

why JESUS CHRIST matters

Group Publishing, Inc.
Attention: Core Belief Talk-back
P.O. Box 481
Loveland, CO 80539
Fax: (970) 669-1994

Please help us continue to provide innovative and useful resources for ministry. After you've led the studies in this volume, take a moment to fill out this evaluation; then mail or fax it to us at the address above. Thanks!

●●●●●●

1. As a whole, this book has been (circle one)

not very helpful								very helpful	
1	2	3	4	5	6	7	8	9	10

2. The best things about this book:

3. How this book could be improved:

4. What I will change because of this book:

5. Would you be interested in field-testing future Core Belief Bible Studies and giving us your feedback? If so, please complete the information below:

Name ______________________________

Street address ______________________________

City ____________________ State ____________ Zip ____________

Daytime telephone (____) ____________________ Date ____________

THANKS!